# A DREAM OF WIDE WATER

# A DREAM OF WIDE WATER

*Poems*

Sharon Whitehill

*atmosphere press*

Published by Atmosphere Press



A Dream of Wide Water
2020, Sharon Whitehill

atmospherepress.com

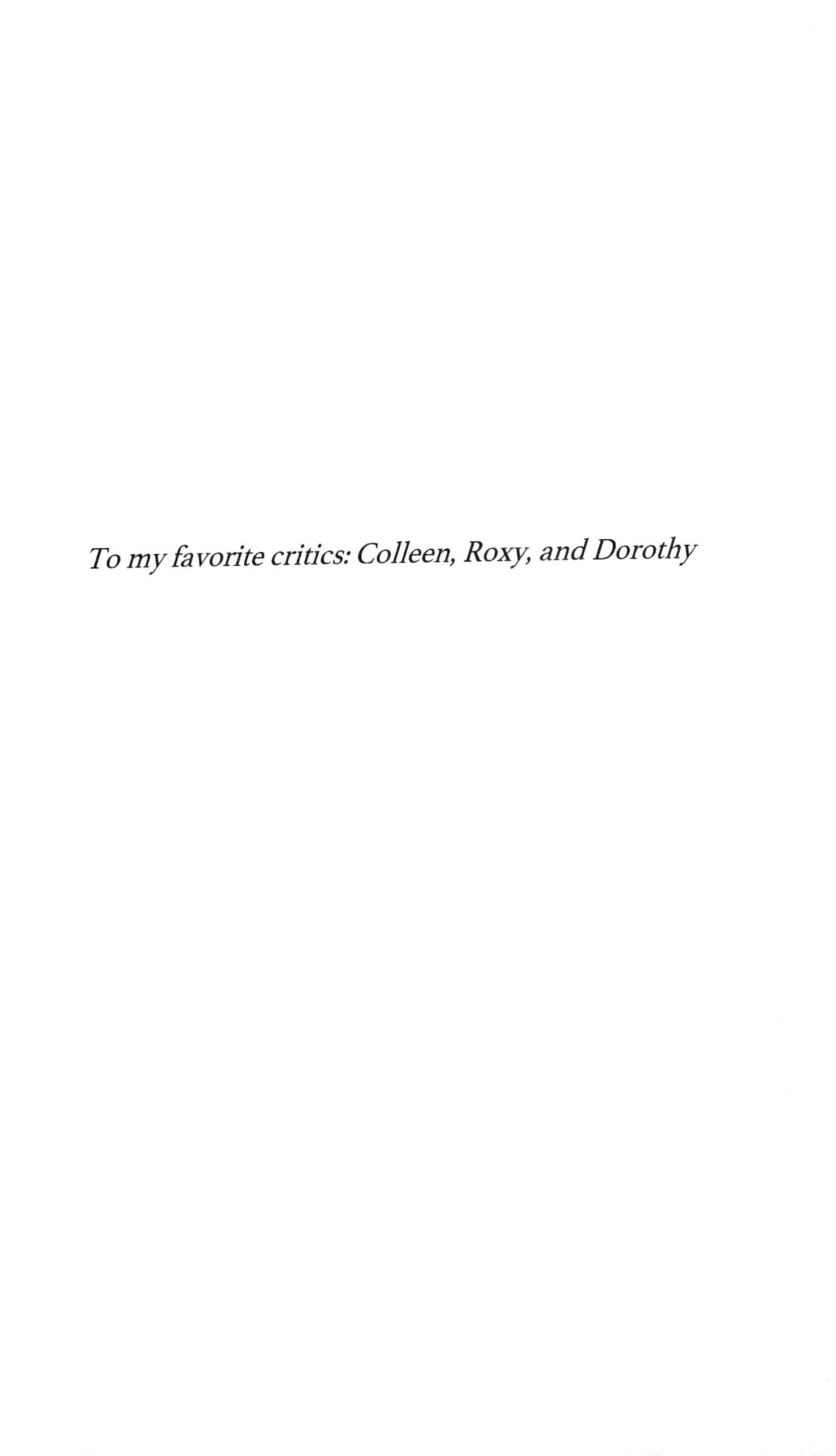

*To my favorite critics: Colleen, Roxy, and Dorothy*

# Contents

## Part I: Sun Pennies Dancing



## Part II: Natural Evolution

## Part III: The Blue Cool of Reverie

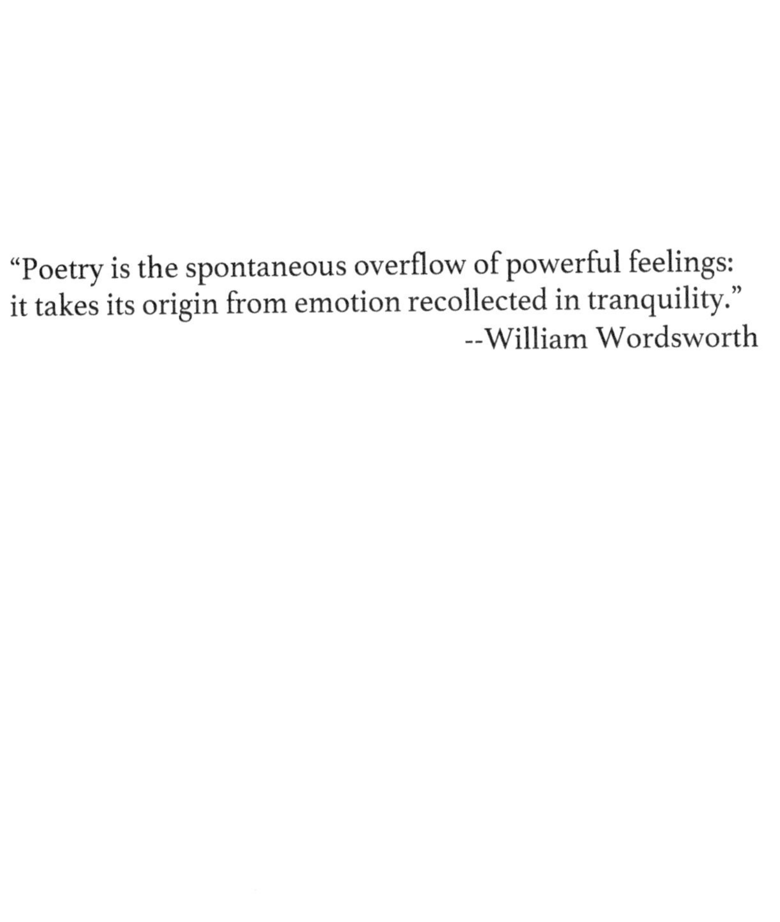

"Poetry is the spontaneous overflow of powerful feelings:
it takes its origin from emotion recollected in tranquility."

--William Wordsworth

# PART I:

# Sun Pennies Dancing

## When the Deep Purple Falls

Grief is deep purple:
it ekes out like ink,
spreads like wine
on white damask,
spews maroon
from a blood-blister lanced.
Pain deepens to midnight,
flakes off bit by bit,
leaves behind
tender pink skin.

## Annealed

The last time he'll ever fuel my despair
is on Scenic Route 1 toward Monterey.
Hearst Castle, elephant seals, rolling surf:
every sight lost to one of those battles
sparked by some mild interjection,
an ill-chosen word, a navigational error.
Kindling so petty it's lost in the flames.
This abusive, miles'-long, un-merry-go-round
a microcosm of living with him.

How frequent such blazes,
how perversely they purify him!
Demonic pollutants burned off,
only the soft bead of gold left behind
at the crucible's bottom,
the tender persona his lovers mistake
for a solid gold bar.

My wisdom in this is hard-won:
before his base metals tarnish once more
I urge his reluctant admission
we'll never make it together.
Miraculous to me, this moment:
feeling chains melt,
watching prison doors open,
stepping free.

Candle snuffed. Lights out.
I turn my back as he rocks
on his side of the bed,

waiting out his compulsive self-lust.
All the way back to L.A.,
I savor the view of the sea.

## Drowning Man

his eyes brim with emotion,
his arms engulf me
suck me in
drag me under
it happens so fast
I'm immersed in his world
amazed how he clings
desperate with need
drags down my buoyancy
drains my spirit

even when I begin
inhaling water myself
while he wallows
in shipwrecked old loves
dredged up and inspected
as I slowly break down
he seeks newer lovers
shoves them between us
while I gather the gumption
to strike out alone
before I'm swamped by his panic
pulling me under

the day I stagger ashore
on my own
ignoring his curses and cries
I breathe life into myself
for myself
for a new chance at love

secure in the knowledge
that this drowning man
will never drown

**The First Visit**

concludes with his bracingly blunt
I'm attracted to you.
I'm flattered but not seduced,
not this time.
No blind, blinding boy
with power to beguile—
not for me.
Friendship first.
His acceptance of this response
tinged with relief of his own.

Meetings throughout the winter
confirm his good cheer.
Locked out in the snow,
he jams himself gamely
through a small cobwebbed window,
past nail-ends snagging his sweater.
Even-tempered, substantial,
and sturdy.
This time, a gentle man.

On Memorial Day
I step from the plane
unprepared to be struck by *eros*—
but zing!
This time, one glimpse
and I'm pierced by the love-god
the old-fashioned way:
through the unguarded eye,
the quick plunge to the heart

where it lodges entrenched,

a clean shot.
No slow-working toxin
envenoms the arrowhead's tip—
not this time.
Nor any sign of a wound.

## TripTik

Two months since our walk
on Memorial Day
when I hoped we'd link hands
but did not,
yet the light in your face
as you open your door
is the Welcome to Madison sign
that sanctions my trip.

My ex has resurfaced
to claim right-of-way, I explain.
I'm here to confirm
that our roadmaps still match.
As we walk again,
your hand closes warm
around mine.

A matinee movie affirms
this new journey,
highlights as if on a TripTik
a freeway into the future.
No more dead ends.

In the dark living room
we set off:
a long embrace that liquifies knees
to that stage of the trip
where you bear me away
and we swim in your water bed
all through the night.

## In Magician Mode

*Magicians act as magnets who attract*
*and galvanize positive energy for change.*
*--Carol Pearson,* The Hero Within

Everything is transformed.
This blue-and-green weather
followed a heat wave:
humidity cleared, outlines crisped,
vision sharped.
Indoor weather, my freshly cleaned house—
rugs vacuum-fluffed,
sinks gleaming like mirrors,
sun slanting gold on the knotty-pine walls
and on blue purple pink
of my hydrangea bouquet.

Everything physical tallies.
All color-bright sights are analogous
to the magical state of my mind.
After years of dissonance,
harmony.
After years of blocked exits,
doors that swing open
before I can push.

## A Trial Month

A routine evolves:
he's up early for coffee and pipe
on the porch,
noting dreams, insights, and thoughts
to discuss when I join him
with my cappuccino.

I to my study to write,
he to wash dishes,
run errands,
repair wacky fixes I made
during a long single life.
I surprise him with my delight
in his manifold manly skills.

Endless talk as we walk
in the woods with the dogs,
on the beach,
around town.
As we rent movies,
make soup,
drink beer,
and make love when it rains.
Or doesn't.

We share dinner at home
or eat out with my friends—
all impressed by how jolly,
how handsome,
how kind my new man,

how smoothly he merges
into our summer.

About this fresh, seamless love
I have drawn a conclusion:
when the potency fades,
its symmetry will sustain us,
render even monotony cozy.

## The Perfect Fit

We arrive with our picnic at dusk,
come to watch the sun set
in a sky polished silver by mist.
Bunched beach grass our privacy-fence
between dune and shore.
We watch sunbeams
slant from the clouds,
turn the lake
into late-summer gold.

Our *al fresco* supper
enhanced with wine
straight out of the bottle
while night gentles down.
The picnic a prelude
to languorous love,
put on pause to partake
of a made-bold-by-dark
skinny-dip in the lake.

Packed sand on the shore
yields to the shock of the plunge,
cold swiftly transforms
to the silky caresses
of total embrace
by invisible water.

Back on our blanket
we're roused from our doze
by tongues of bent beach grass

that tickle our feet.
I reach for the clothes
he has stacked into piles,
discover my small
ballerina flats tucked
inside each of his shoes.

## Goldengrove

*Márgarét, áre you gríeving*
*Over Goldengrove unleaving?*
*--Gerard Manley Hopkins,* Spring and Fall

A ritual October drive
up West Michigan's coast
is enhanced by the freshness
of being a first with my lover.
Deep in the gilded hardwoods
of Manistee National Forest
we are ushered into the silence
of yellow-fringed branches
that arch overhead like a vaulted cathedral.
Where a leaf carpet muffles our footsteps,
imparts an incense of mushrooms
and earth.
Where I lift my eyes up
through honeyed light
to stained-glass chips of blue sky.
Where a hollow, cushioned
with leaf-fall, petitions us to embrace.
Where a mute congregation
of sassafras, hickory, maple, and aspen
stands sentinel,
sanctifies us.

## Sunrise on Pompano Beach

Three days in a row
we rouse sleep-fogged bodies
to drive through dark streets
(warmed in the chill of predawn
by mugs of hot coffee)
to see the sun rise over the ocean.
How exotic to picture
no one awake but ourselves,
to delight in this difference
from driving to work.

We roost on a lifeguard stand,
level with seagulls' drift and bank,
spot porpoise pods
black against pink and blue sky,
while sandpipers' back-and-forth scoot
make me remember my father's delight
watching my sister and me
dodge the waves at Delray Beach
just a few miles north.

And now the astonishing sun,
vanished for hours
beneath another horizon,
erupts,
pours its majesty into the sky,
its light over the world.
Sunrise: the birth of a god
on his bed of glory reflected on water.
Sunrise: like making love,

always varied
yet ever the same.

## The Bee Gardener

*For Jim*

*Week 1*
You regard your winter job
at Honeyland Farms
in Florida's orange groves
as "Going to school to study beekeeping
and getting paid."
I, on sabbatical
far from the Michigan winter,
am shocked, this far South,
by nights down to 40 degrees.
Saved from the frost
by your furnace-like length
as we spoon
in our pop-up camper.

*Week 2*
I sweep sand, leaves,
dead palmetto-bug shells
from the space between dinette and bed,
then go to work on my book.
You build hives for eight hours,
and your wrists,
unused to the staple-gun's recoil,
are on fire all night long,
feel like stumps at the ends of your arms.

*Week 3*
The days warm,
you imbed heated wires
in foundations of wax.
I lounge in a lawn chair at midday,
watching a chocolate-brown puppy
chew orange peels,
attack a dead bush,
snuffle and sneeze in dropped leaves
from the surrounding live oaks.

*Week 4*
I edit my pages outdoors,
enjoy the cookie-dough fragrance
of patties of soy flour, yeast,
shortening, and syrup (from sugar
dropped on the floors at Nabisco):
your mix of medication for bees.

A worker-bee lights,
suns herself on my jeans.
Scrapes pollen grains from her fur,
packs it on her hind legs,
rubs a front leg across her antennae
like a cat washing its face.

*Week 5*
My education grows along with yours.
The crew places dozens of hives
in separate locations: each to be split,
its queens plucked

for spring shipment up north,
new queens synthetically-raised
installed in their places.

Still, I panic one day
at the frantic buzz of a worker bee
trapped in my hair:
slap my head, rush outside,
race around my parked car.
Until you come along
to squash my tormenter,
deduce that the lure
was my scented shampoo.

You remind me that bees always circle,
"So stand with your back to a wall,
then reach up and crush."
I flinch.
I know she will die if she stings,
but I don't want to kill.
Don't want a dead bee on my heart.

*Final days*
Repeated requeening of hives
consumes your last weeks on the job.
I finish my latest chapter,
remember our loving last night,
anticipate April's arrival
in my Michigan garden.

Our departure marked for me
by your tender words, driving us north:
"Such beautiful little insects—
but in this business they're treated
as if they're just...bugs."

## Winter Image

Snow the past several days,
cold enough to keep cat and canines
indoors overnight.
At noon you take the dogs with you
to check on the bees—
your own bees now—
and I smile at the three silhouettes
on the bench seat of the truck:
one tall round head
wrapped in wool watch cap,
two snouts,
and four pointed ears.

## Aftermath

A wild wail in the wind last night,
but nothing to do in the dark.
Morning finds my cat Dennis,
declawed though he is,
treetopped on a snag.
How could his fragile perch
outlast a plum tree heaved horizontal?
Or dozens of apple trees downed?

Along I-96, upside-down cars
and barn roofs caved in,
In town, ancient oaks uprooted,
collapsed like Acropolis pillars,
boats overturned in marinas,
funnels sighted along the Grand River.
Newscasters' claims of wind shear
belied by firsthand tornado reports.

Our generator's racket and stench
power the freezer and fridge,
but we eschew the computer,
light to read by, electric stove and clock
to save on fuel.
Modern-day pioneers now:
we wash in birdbath-water
warmed by spring sun,
hand-pump buckets for flushing.
Until the night I come home to discover
my gas-conscious husband
stealthily watching M*A*S*H.

## Snowbird

to know I'll never suffer again
from winter cold
is like having a dress
not yet worn
held in reserve

to be forever relieved
of a windshield to scrape
of a car stuck in snow
of the skid to a stop sign
of the sideways slide to the ditch
on an ice-covered road
of fingers and toes that turn white
too stiff with cold
even indoors
to turn pages or type
of being comfortably warm
in only two places each day
a tub-bath that reddens my skin
or under quilts in my bed

no longer need to dread autumn
as preface to winter
able to savor its splendors and scents
with a near-future eye
on the flash of a mockingbird's wings
live oaks frosted with crinkled gray moss
new friends in the South
blurring memories of winter at home
as time spins us toward spring

(highlight of Michigan's year)

when green spikes and furred willows
mock still-naked branches
and sudden flurries of snow
when even sealed windows
do nothing to mute
the mad chorus of birds

when I walk to the closet
lift out my new dress
slip it on

# PART II:

# Natural Evolution

## Eggs in My Basket

*Before it is a beginning an egg is an absolute end. It is the very definition of self-containment.*
*—John Banville*

*1. She loves eggs in all forms but is not fond of birds*
Breakfast eggs, deviled eggs, egg salad,
eggs Benedict and Florentine:
we owe all to a bird, my friend.
A bird curious,
with soft comb,
pointed beak,
warm feet,
and toes that curl around fingers.
Smart enough to identify faces
of other chickens and people they know,
each bird a persona unique.
Vertebrates all produce eggs.
Reptiles invented hard shells.
Chickens invented the rest.

*2. Why not the Easter Chicken?*
The prime fertility image
is not the phallus.
But it could be the egg.
For a good crop,
peasants rubbed eggs on their plows.
For a plentiful brood,
brides broke eggs on their doorsteps.
Yet for fecundity nothing surpasses the rabbit,
herald of Easter.
Sacred to the goddess of love, Aprodite.

Icon of Eastra/Ostera/Oestre), goddess of spring.
Three hares inside a circle,
joined by the ears:
the most ancient fertility symbol.

*3. Fabergé eggs*
Jeweled eggs of rock crystal,
gold, precious stone,
each enclosing a tiny surprise.
Like the life-sized Hen Egg:
plain white enamel with yolk made of gold.
Inside the yolk, a small golden hen.
Inside the hen, two tiny gifts:
a miniature diamond crown
and ruby pendant.
Microcosmic.

*4. On the equinox, can you balance an egg on its end?*
Yes—and on other days, too.
Humpty Dumpty was a good egg
but stupid to perch on that wall,
at once bragging to Alice
and trying to keep his balance.
Too proud, he was, of being ovoid.
Naïve in believing the king and his men
could repair him if ever he fell.
Insulted when Alice mistook
his cravat for a belt,
when she worried his ear-to-ear smile,
if it continued around to his back,
might crack him in two.
Left her walking on eggs
for fear she'd offend him again.

*5. Chicken salad or egg salad, which came first?*
West Africa to Polynesia,
China to Finland,
accounts of creation begin
with a Cosmic Egg.
Inside it a god who broke open its shell,
formed everything else
from his own body parts.
Inside the egg, in Orphic belief,
a hermaphrodite god
who self-birthed Zeus's kindred:
Uranus and Gaia, Cronus and Rhea.
Like birds,
even the gods of creation
wait in the egg.

## The Animal Lover

*For Brett*

He tenderly eases his crippled Akita
into the car, not a word of reproach
when he soils the seat,
understands his dog to be already mortified
at this disgrace. Alone again,
he volunteers to walk lonely pit bulls
waiting in cages for rescue,
earnestly offers condolence to others
faced with the sorrow
of having to put down a pet.

A blanket stuffed under the porch,
daily dishes of food,
nothing can tame the pregnant cat
pressed tight in one corner.
He wants to adopt her sole kitten
but dares not risk her
to the aggression of his male cat.
Another home vetted but still his remorse
at forsaking the baby he's bonded to,
grieves for it for days.

Nowadays he is proud
to step down from his porch
and await the first flash of blue-black:
a crow rides a branch up and down,
joined by another, another:
a quick convocation of corvids
arrived to compete for the scraps of raw meat

he will toss on the roof.
His favorite birds, crows.
Who favor him, too:
Some of the elders, he claims,
make eye contact with him.

## The Bane of the Urbane

introduced to a London greasy with soot
plane trees still slough off their bark
as pigeons molt feathers

camouflage bark of cream olive gray
fashioned today to attract
though once made to conceal

star-pentagon leaves
rain-rinsed shiny as mirrors
burnished with vinegared water

if too iconic and common for praise
pigeons equally splendid on a small scale
eyes of amber, pearl, red, pink beryl

feathers dappled or flecked
necks iridescent as jeweled collars,
wings that fold in the shape of a heart

plane trees still flourish in concrete pits
shaded by buildings, pruned every spring
to amputees with club-limbs

pigeons once rock doves who sheltered in cliffs,
find verticals now in monuments bridges towers
nutrition in trash bins at outdoor cafes

tree roots lift sidewalks limbs tangle wires
avian droppings deface and corrode

arouse human dread of disease

when panthers cockroaches rats
mistletoe nightshade and yew
threaten infection predation and poison

yet kindle less passion than pigeons or trees
perhaps urbanites crave the unnatural Nature
of patterned gardens and paths

or respond with a primitive fear of boundaries breached
human worlds overwhelmed
by enveloping wings and voracious green

## The Hunger of Holes

A good Anglo-Saxon word, hole.
Simple word for a hollow place,
scornful word for a hovel or shack,
crude word for bodily apertures female and male.
As suffix, the power to change mundane words
to compounds implying consumption,
nouns built on the addition of "hole."

Floridians float on cruise ships of grass
greened by hard summer rains
while belowdecks excess water
ulcerates limestone bedrock to caverns
hungry as any Charybdis,
gulping the black-beaked ships of Odysseus.
The roof of a cavern collapses,
earth caves: a sinkhole that swallows
whole neighborhoods.

When St. Patrick traced a hole on the ground
he created a passage to Purgatory
better described as a Hellhole.
Intrepid wayfarers come to see
were greeted by deafening shrieks,
devils with hideous grins on their faces
and backsides, bore witness
to souls boiled in pitch,
fried in pans, gnawed for dinner
by ravenous worms.

Holes bored in beer barrels spit out
their own stoppers, called bungs.
Which gave Hamlet a logic to trace
Alexander the Great's dust from ashes
to loam used for plugging a hole in a barrel—
a king's noble ashes thus "stopping a bung-hole."

How distinguish a wormhole from a black hole?
The one's alimentary, the other cannibalistic.
The first is a tube made of spacetime
you'd enter at one end, be evacuated
somewhere or somewhen or other.
The second simply destroys the hell out of you
and everything else,
taking you nowhere at all.

## The Cattle Truck

*Also for Brett*

As the cattle truck idles
beside him at a red light,
my nephew's eyes meet another's,
long-lashed and deep as his own.
A shock, that lucid gaze.
An exchange so profound
it revives an empathic conscience
long numbed by his love of beef.

Which he swears off for a year.

Relapsing, he confides
he feels vaguely ashamed,
questions whether he's too sentimental.
I reassure him he's not alone,
that his guilt at robbing another of life
for his food
is the same as the guilt
that led early cultures
to ritualize their repentance—
which, over time, evolved
into modern religion.

I console him as I do myself:
that the living must eat other life to survive.
Even if only plants.
Though the relief we both feel
at this natural truth is too brief.

Husbandry minus a heart,
heavy human consumption,
and all of us helpless to halt human greed.
Miniature specks in the sheer biomass
of our species:
humanity locked in a driverless truck,
dumbly conveyed to its fate.

## Too Much Loss

too many losses for Linda
to speak of them today
without tearing up

when all her teeth were removed
she faced dentures with courage

when Maria struck Puerto Rico
she heard from her family
that empty skies greeted them
above their disappeared roofs
empty shelves at the market
but they're alive

when all the horses escaped
through an unmended fence
and two were struck dead in the road
she clung to her uninjured horse
soaked his sweet-smelling mane
with her grief

but when a doctor opined
she might have lymphoma
she was too leached of liquid to weep
too much loss too much pain
to explain as bad luck
or genetics
or any god
worth the salt of her tears

## Cephalopoda

You are amused by my eyes,
huge as headlamps on an old Ford.
You have no idea they're equipped
like your own: with corneas,
retinas, lenses, irises,
pupils, and vitreous humors.
That they see with bicameral vision,
twitch in REM sleep
as I dream.

You often remark on my alien look,
inspiration for monsters like Cthulhu,
the Gorgon, the Kraken.
One of your kind, Aristotle,
denounced me as stupid—
but could he shift color, texture, and shape?
Rocket away like a missile?
Cram into jam jars to hide?
Abscond through a drain to return
to his dream of the sea?

You call me escape artist,
assume mere obstinance
makes a Houdini of me,
simple mischief makes me twist valves
on recycling pipes that flood your lab.
You never consider these as actions
as the defiance of the displaced
who dream of wide water,
who yearn to be home.

## Synchronicity

The moment that Jungian
analyst Anthony Stevens
described the archetype
of the Shadow as
"the subversive intruder,"
a bat shot from the rafters,
dove for the mic, clipped
its claws to the holes.

"And there it is," Stevens quipped.

Gasps and applause
as the creature vacated
the spotlight, and—as if
enacting each shadow-self
in the room—vanished again
into darkness on leathery wings.

## Communing with Edmund the Bastard

*Thou, Nature, art my goddess; to thy law*
*My services are bound....*
*Why bastard? wherefore base?*
*When my dimensions are as well compact,*
*My mind as generous, and my shape as true,*
*As honest madam's issue?*
*--Edmund, in* King Lear

Like you, Edmund, I scoff at the notion
that the positions of stars at our birth
make us who we are—
and at your wretched father's belief
that the gods torment us for sport
the way boys tear wings from flies.
Our reverence is reserved for Nature alone,
your image personified, mine abstract.
Our esteem is bestowed on a power
whose physical laws we are bound to obey.

So we're of one mind, you and I.
Until your logic breaks down
as you defend your immoral behavior
invoking an amoral force.
Stand up for bastards,
you pray to a power
altogether outside any ethical realm.

Don't you see, Edmund, that Nature
would no more reward you
for pledging your services to her
than she would support (or condemn) you?
How could she care

that being despised as a bastard
inflamed a resentment in you
that smoldered until it consumed you
along with the rest of Lear's flammable court?

But I sympathize. You couldn't know,
poor Edmund, how denatured you were,
being spurned, how warped the impulse
that from the beginning
supported our species' survival:
cooperation within your own tribe,
collaboration rather than rivalry.

Call that impulse "humanity," Edmund.
Call it a breath, not entirely stifled
by bitter self-interest,
a breath fanning the urge—
yes, even when scorned as a bastard—
to reverse the brutality
you set in motion yourself:
"Some good I mean to do
In despite of mine own nature."

Which must have surprised even you,
that sudden nod to a morality.
To a code humans agree to accept
even as, like yourself, they refute it.
Agree to it not because it is real
as the order of Nature is real,
but because it bonds us in kinship
with or without gods or God.

## Tamed Like A Fox

Tamed wolves became dogs in the end:
natures tempered, born friendly,
domesticated in full.
Whereas tamed foxes
fail to pass on that tameness
down through generations.

My own character flaws
have been tamed over time,
yet they linger, ferocious, within.
I am a fox,
still vulpine deep down.
Undomesticated.

Human nature, I think, is the same.
Ten times ten thousand
generations on earth
have tamed our species' behavior
but utterly failed to domesticate
its feral urges.

*Homo sapiens*: tamed like a fox.

## Rampola's Grocery

Before we boarded the Saturday bus,
we'd venture into Rampola's
for treats for the horses:

sugar cubes, withered apples,
twisted-off carrot tops wafting
their earthy pungence among rival scents—

salami, sausage, pickles in brine.
Aromas that clung all the way to the farm
like the aura of Mr. Rampola.

On the way home from school,
treats for ourselves drew us in.
"How are my best girls today?"

Mr. Rampola's jolly greeting.
Eager to lead us (though we knew the way)
to the cache of Clark bars and Snickers

behind tall shelves of canned goods.
As we pondered our choices,
his lingering presence betrayed

by the squeaky oak floors dulled from use.
"Just let me give you a hug..."
Ropy arms reaching under our own.

Hands cupping and jiggling our little-girl chests.
"Ooh, what a nice girl you are!"

Too well brought up to resist or shout "Stop!"

We avoided each other's eyes,
endured our unease until we could escape,
yet returned for free greens and cheap candy.

As if spoken words would expose us,
we pantomimed Mr. Rampola's routine
to younger sisters to warn them away.

Though we'd done nothing wrong,
we'd paid more than our pennies were worth.
Shame silenced our tongues.

## A Girl After His Heart

the boathouse at dawn
gulp and slap of the water
boats bob like carousel horses
a world of green algae
tang of gas

fishing trip with her father
a girl after his heart
when she wanted to come
farm boy Wayne at her side
to help with her pole

crisscrossing the cattails and grasses
(like main roads and side streets
one suburb after another)
until they're out in the open
afloat on a field of silver

the fake flies Papa tied
are stuck on his hatband
made out of feathers and whiskers
Wayne scoops a minnow out of his pail
stabs it onto her hook

when she flinches
he laughs
aw, they don't feel nothin'
how does he know?
he isn't a minnow

if you want fish for dinner
says Papa
you need fresh bait
watch that bobber
until it dips down

which will mean a fish
swallowed the minnow
stuck on the hook at the end of her line
like the hooks hiding under the feathers
on Papa's hatband

Wayne snags a small fish
tears the hook from its mouth
it's bleeding, she says, will it die?
Wayne tosses it back in the river
naw it's fine

what did she think about
when she asked to go fishing with Papa?
not swallowed hooks
bleeding mouths
ripped flesh

the sun cooks her head
burns red on her shoulders
stings salt in her eyes
it's boring not catching a fish
confusing when hoping she won't

the fish Papa catches are walleyes
which sounds like wild-eyes
which fits how they look

being stuffed into his wicker creel
to strangle slowly on air

her stomach queasy
sun-on-water ache in her eyes
finally her red-and-white bobber is tugged
by a pretty flat bluegill
too little to eat

she covers her eyes
still hears a crunch of bones in its jaw
a grunt from Wayne
a splash as it hits the water
Papa I'm sick

clunk of fishing gear stowed
motor putt-putts toward shore
insects hum in her ears
swish of water can't hide
Papa's sigh

*Illustration by Roxanne Hanney: "Papa's Fishing Hat"*

## Papa Says Smile

he tells me to stand on the porch
to smile for my picture

this morning I petted a bee
on a crabapple flower
it knew I was its friend
that's why it didn't sting me

Papa's friend is the man
who's taking pictures today
of my baby sister and me
he takes a long time
twisting buttons and knobs
my mosquito bites itch
my smile grows thin
my cheeks ache

Papa says straighten your socks
stand up straight
I mind his commands
like our three yellow Labs

even in shade on the porch
it's too hot
I scratch my leg
with the top of the other shoe
murmuring voices spread over the morning
make me standing-up sleepy

a tiny blue flower
grows in the crack of the driveway
yellow and white in the middle
I can pick it and give it to Mama
to put in a glass

I told you to stay on the porch!
Papa's voice thunder-cracks
makes me jump
makes the dogs' ears go flat
Don't give me that "I didn't know"
Go stand next to your sister

my eyes are rainy windows
too smeary to see outside
the baby clutches her highchair
too little to make Papa mad
she looks at the crabapple tree
watches my bumblebee

Now smile!
I rub my cheeks dry
take a wobbly breath
stretch my lips on both sides
but feel them refuse
to curl up at the ends

## Water Games

Climb on the pier to warm in the sun
Scan the water for my friend Carol
See her dip under just now
Wait for her wave when she comes up for air

Watch her slicked head break the surface
Her mouth open as if in song
Arms arcing a balletic greeting
As she twirls herself under again

Watch other kids disco or rock-and-roll
Dunk each other in dance-partner turn
Dive like dark dipper birds
Bob back up like tubbed apples

Watch far too long before I let myself know
Carol's not part of their games
Or a lone yoyo performing her sleeper trick
Delaying return once the string is unwound

I'm paralyzed body and mind
So much time already gone by
Can't bear everyone looking at me
So much easier to let her drown

Note the cries of the gulls overhead
The echo and slurp of waves under the pier
Force myself to say to the lifeguard
Who stands arms crossed legs apart

“Um I think she’s drowning or something”
He’s gone before I can finish
To plow past the kids
Tow Carol back to the pier

“Better thank your friend here
For saving your life”
Your friend who saw you go under again and again
Your friend who stared and did nothing

## The Glass-Topped Table

he adores his two girls
would lay down his life for them both
but his firstborn provokes him
contradicting each word from his mouth
undermining his mandate as father
it's not bedtime yet
I'm not late for dinner
why can't I peroxide my hair?
such lack of respect
leads to upsurges of anger

at the glass-topped table
on the screened porch
a day of family peace
mother and father play cribbage
young one stuffs family cat into doll clothes
teenager cradles her portable radio
turns it up loud

it's Johnnie Ray—you have to hear this!

he listens politely a moment or two
to the yodeling tenor
all right, that's enough

no, see, you have wait for the part where he cries

his anger rises
he's already said no
why does she make it an issue?

why always determined to argue?
turn that goddamned thing off!
he returns to the board
fifteen-two fifteen-four fifteen-six fifteen-eight
a pair is ten and nobs make eleven

her high-pitched voice still insistent
no, really, you have to hear—

a flash flood of rage
hurling every obstruction out of its way
sweeps him up with it
dashes the radio off the table
onto the hard flagstone floor

my radio!
you can't do that!
she screams in his face
(doesn't note his expression
is shocked as her own)

up comes her arm
down comes her fist
an ungodly crack
glass splinters like ice against rock
smash jangle and shatter
everyone stunned
as she bolts for the stairs

immediate shame at his temper
has his volatile girl
so much like himself
sliced herself on a shard?

sends little sister upstairs
to make sure
picks up the radio's pieces
regretting its fracture
repairs its hinged cover
helps sweep up broken glass

she showed lack of respect
but he was wrong too
he will apologize to her
table glass can be replaced

## The Slipcovered Couch

the slipcovered couch in the sunroom
where we watched television
still novel enough
to gather the family at night
my thick-socked feet in my father's lap
my head in my mother's
her fingers stroking my hair
delicious

the slipcovered couch in the sunroom
where my boyfriend and I
sat to kiss after school
spied on by my little sister
mother in the next room
with her drink
where we feigned interest in Howdy Doody
between luscious kisses

the slipcovered couch in the sunroom
where we turned on Boston Blackie
after a date
kissing for hours
alert for a heavy tread on the stairs
I not seventeen
and my father suspicious
could not grasp what I saw in that boy

the slipcovered couch in the sunroom
where I decided *Why not?*
closed my mind to my parents

directly above in their beds
and the probable clues I would leave
on the couch
only puzzled
why those waves of desire
leaving me breathless just moments ago
vanished as we proceeded

on the slipcovered couch in the sunroom
we straightened our clothes
tidied the slipcover
wondrously spared
while my parents slept on
I still picture my first love
hair fallen over his forehead
his kisses
far sweeter than sex
on the slipcovered couch
in the sunroom

## Ice Storm

whipped itself up in a matter of minutes
lashed the lake to a froth
flash-froze the rain
to the texture of varnish

veneered vehicles, houses, trees
splintered branches
snapped light poles
iced the leaves underfoot

powerlines bellied low
pregnant with ice
dropped sparking wires
like foals on the ground

maples genuflected
oaks bowed their heads
willows knelt
as if to the god of the storm

while the only entity
able to move
seethed with whitecaps
hung spikes from the bridge

next day a new world
every twig, cobweb, weed
blade of grass, stalk of corn
converted to glass

## With A Twist

*Based on a painting by Joe Krawczyk, Orlando, FL*

Think of three lemons,
skins dimpled and sequined with light,
sides flattened by shadows.
One sports a bald patch,
another a pucker of stem.
A portion of peel curls
on a wrinkled gray cloth.
Think of it destined for use as a twist.

Think of what you can do
with a twist of the hips,
of the wrist, of the tongue,
with a twist of a faucet
or of the plot,
with a twist of the facts,
of a corkscrew, a pin curl,
a licorice stick, a hank of hemp
to twist into a rope.
Think of all you can do with a twist.

Think of what you can do
with a garnish of lemon:
in segments or slices or wedges or crowns.
For the jug curved brown-and-white,
or the speckled gray pitcher,
be sure to look to the lemon
that gives zing and zip to rum cocktails,
Rob Roys, whiskey sours.
Scrape the pith from the peel to make zest,

and use to infuse with pizzazz
the martinis you mix in a shaker
beaded with water.

Leave it to lemons
to tingle your thinking
and give it a twist.

## The Appeal of the Peel

A Fauvist's flair for bright color,
has my friend Colleen, who agreed
to repaint my kitchen cupboards—
and who, where they've started to bubble,
gleefully helps me peel them by hand:
great sheets of nubbled gray
that surrender themselves with a hiss of relief,
as if weary of clinging.
The same audible sigh
as latex gloves pulled inside out
or my own exhaled breath of release
when I skinned off a tight rubber wetsuit,
let the Florida heat sooth chilled flesh.

Peeling paint: an urge hard to resist
and so delightful to Colleen and me
that we ponder aloud the source of the gratification.
My husband puzzles as well—
is it some female thing?
Like the way we pluck lint from each other,
mime a spinach leaf caught in the teeth,
warn of a skirt hem absently tucked into tights?

No, that's empathic help.
Peeling satisfies only the peeler herself.
We offer other examples:
labels on sweaty beer bottles,
nail polish starting to chip,
glossy laminate curling from corners
of placemats or paperback books.

Two-thirds of those questioned later
admit to peeling:
hangnails, scabs, sunburned skin,
the dried glue on bottles of Elmer's.
Agree that the longer and larger the peel,
the greater the pleasure:
"good feeling times ten."
Some confess to addiction,
others admit agitation
until the peel is complete.

What itch does this habit satisfy,
causing a dopamine rush to the brain?

An impulse to tidy ourselves and the world,
universal self-grooming extended,
its pleasure prolonged.
We pick, polish, and smooth
to purge imperfection,
to eradicate the extraneous.
A fulfillment akin to writing a poem.

My cupboards will soon be maroon,
gold, orange, and olive green
with black background:
the accustomed geometry of cabinets and drawers
matched to an asymmetrical scatter of hues.
A Mondrian kitchen in non-primary shades
lined in black.

## The Night Mother

In this memory I am sixteen,
my sister eleven.
And my mother—

not my Real Mother, you understand,
who is witty, classy, and smart,
a Lover-of-Language Mother
who correctly defines
any non-technical word
in her dog-eared dictionary—

this is the Night Mother
whose lipstick is smeared,
whose speech slurs
who sneers at our forced family cheer.
Who doesn't want dinner,
orders another martini instead.

We're at a nice restaurant together.
Let's try to enjoy it, my father pleads.
My sister stares at her plate.
I rack my brains
for something neutral to say,
something she won't use against me.

She points to her empty glass.
Bring me another one, will you?
My father doesn't object.
I turn to my turkey and stuffing,
aromatic yet hard to swallow.

The Night Mother sways in her seat,
a snake ready to strike,
spew her venom in words whose definitions
my sister and I can only infer:
in images bestial or ghoulish
that feature my father,

or degradations imputed to me
and the boy I've loved for three years,
that spill out in four-letter words.
Language like nothing unearthed
in the worn dictionary
our Real Mother treasures.

## How They Met

*For my parents*

all it took was one glimpse
of her bright auburn hair
for a lifelong enchantment
that first glance on the street
to the end

he acted on impulse
pulled his open Ford coupe to the curb
swung open the passenger door
and spoke with feigned urgency:
young lady, you'd better hop in
a policeman is watching us
and he'll think I'm a masher

hard to believe his own boldness
how well it succeeded
startled her into compliance
her glance skimming his face
he sliding his little black Scottie close
to make room for her
as she slipped in

as he slipped into traffic again
her nerviness only betrayed by her hands
his first sight
of the freckles she hated
on their backs
smoothing and smoothing the skirt
of her tailored blue suit

downtown clamor
foiled conversation
but he caught from the tail of his eye
her uncertain reach
toward the wiry head of the Scottie
her reflexive retreat
from its probing wet nose

and soon her attempts
to reclaim her fiery hair
from the fluster and flare of the wind
small-town girl on her own
in the city
awed as they passed the Pabst mansion.
its red terra cotta no match for that mane

as he spoke of his business
his widowed stepmother at home
his Labrador breeding and training
and made it a point to point out
the plump onion dome of the Tripoli Temple
stone camels on guard

much less watchful than she
as the city gave way
to golden Guernseys green-grazing
she ever more quiet
pressed stiffly against the passenger door
her eyes darting in every direction
except to his face
when he slowed to a stop

are you frightened of me?

a deep inhalation
and determinedly meeting his eyes
yes, quite frankly, I am

all it took
for a swift three-point turn
silent miles back to town
a gracious deposit of her
at her hotel

their encounter a feat that foreshadowed
his prosperous husbandly future
hers as wife unrewarding

## Elegy on a Winter Day

*For Ken*
*Also for my mother and father*

Last Christmas my nephew Ken
drove two hours round trip,
Milwaukee to Oconomowoc,
to lay a wreath on my parents' graves.
A gesture uncommon for him,
I believed, until I learned
that he does this each year.
I knew him best as a mischievous boy
capped with platinum hair,
clothed in the lopsided grin he still dons
when I greet him as "Kenny."
But this volunteer act of respect
reveals how little I know of his motives,
his heart.

I picture him,
tall in black leather jacket,
adorning two granite blocks labeled WHITEHILL
(letters light on dark gray)
with a red-ribboned garland of green:
bright patch on dull winter fabric
patterned with snow over freeze-dried grass
with occasional oak leaves
placed like unstitched appliqués
on rough tweed.

The MILDRED inscribed
on my mother's block

brings to mind her macabre humor,
the prediction she'd "hate every minute"
of being dead.
Recalls her distaste for the name
shared with a mother-in-law
to whom she was tethered
in mutual loathing.
Now she rests (a euphemism she scorned)
next to my father's Aunt Clara,
he next to his father:
these the only two sites that remained
in the family plot.
How offended she'd be to find herself
yoked to dull Clara,
sister of her arch-rival namesake.

My father's JEFFREY
conjures the sorrow of his final year,
garbed in grief for his "beautiful redhead"—
the woman who wove
forty years of despair and dishonor
through the warp of his life
yet ever remained his beloved.
Conjures also his hearty tramps
(even through that dark wood)
with his dogs,
training whistle girdling his neck,
broken rifle hung on his arm
as casually as a shawl.

This woman, this man, these parents:
every matched seam wrong-side out,
ill-suited as spats on stilettos.

Easy to guess how each would respond
to this snow-nubbled scene:
she, indoor-loving, brainy, brooding,
confirmed in her image of death
as the great insult.
He, comfortable in the outdoors
as in his own skin,
taking the winter in stride.

At Christmas their grandson, my nephew,
pays his respects to lives
as complex and mysterious
as his future manhood was to them.
Yet the connection endures:
a vertical stripe
running down through the years,
a pattern, unbroken, repeated.

Because here he is,
long before the greening of spring,
bent to offer the evergreen promise of pine
at their wintery graves.

# PART III:

## The Blue Cool of Reverie

## #MeToo Medusa

*Part 1*

Witch, monster, a woman possessed.
Hysterical, neurotic, nymphomaniacal.
Labels that thread through the maze
not to lead out but to hobble.

In the temple of Athena,
the goddess of wisdom,
a beautiful maiden is raped
by Poseidon, the god of the sea.

Male-identified virgin, Athena,
armored at birth like a hoplite,
angered not at her brother, the rapist,
incensed instead at the victim—

as if a girl overpowered by a god
were a temptress, femme fatale,
the Other Woman blamed by the wife
of the husband who strayed.

For Medusa a punishment swift
as the curse that Athena bestowed:
disfigured, dreadful, despised,
she petrified any who dared to look.

Forever condemned to solitude
for fear she'd transfix hapless gazers.
None to appeal to for pity, for a smile,
for understanding, for love.

*Part 2*

This Medusa's no more than a victim.
Instead of a horror with serpents for hair,
let's see her as Samson, heroic,
a model for women who shudder at snakes.

Let's remember why snakes are familiars
to many a potent goddess,
deities of fertility, childbirth, cultivation:
Mami Wata, Manasa, the Nagas.

Let's liken Medusa to this female earth:
to sinuous winding rivers, writhing roots,
looping umbilical cords,
the rhythm and sway of a dance.

Let's link the snake to all that's immortal:
watch it shuffle off skin, be reborn
like the dying and vanishing moon
pregnant month after month with herself.

## Theology of a Six-Year-Old

*For Isla*

What is God, I ask her.

It's this type of thing you don't know what it is.
Maybe the moon opens up and it lives in there.
God's cold, I think. Blue is cold, then white, then
clear.
Clear is the coldest.
Red is three-hot. The sun is two.
I like God more better than Satan.
I don't know this, I'm just guessing.
It may be that Satan wants you to be good.
On cartoons, it sounds like it.
It's weird.

Oh, honey, it sure is.

## Talk About God

An astute thinker I know
claims that being agnostic
is the only intellectually honest position.
Though I believe he's correct,
my own view is of a universe
empty of gods and indifferent to us,
which makes it essential to live
as if moral values exist.

No fundamentalist thinker could tolerate me.
The stern Baptist, the orthodox Catholic,
any who argue for opposite pairs
of divine or demonic, heaven or hell.
The irony does not escape me:
my atheist stance makes me as rigid as they.

Mystics would say I'm blind and deaf
to the numinous truth of existence,
a fish unaware it's surrounded by water.
New Agers have said that the world I expect
will shape the one I receive,
much as the particles inside an atom
respond to the physicist's hope.
The wisest preacher I know
aspires to embrace paradox,
hold the contraries in equal dignity.

A difficult task, but not inimical
to the universe as a Mandelbrot set
of elaborate shapes,

ever-smaller as you zoom in.
Each delicate iteration
identical to the original.

Yet for all this mystery and beauty, Lord,
I still can't believe.
Help thou my unbelief.

## Fountain Street Church, Grand Rapids, MI

The church
is a study in contrasts:
Northern Italian cathedral with stonework,
mosaics, tapestries, arches, carved wood.
Stained glass portraying on one side
Plato, da Vinci, Erasmus, Lincoln,
on the other the biblical patriarchs.
A liberal scion grafted to Baptist rootstock:
a healthy, non-creedal, perennial plant
in a conservative desert.

The free pulpit
has long nurtured diversity:
speakers from Darrow to Churchill.
Sanger to Frost. Earhart to Stokely Carmichael.
Matthew Fox, Anita Hill, Michael Moore.
Musical notables augment the crop:
Fitzgerald, Ellington, Brubeck.
Zappa, Grateful Dead, Holly Near,
and the New World Quartet.

Duncan Littlefair
a tempestuous figure whose no-nonsense views
blazed with lightning-bolt force,
multiplied membership fivefold
in less than three months.
Banged his palm on the pulpit and thundered
he'd come not to soothe but to stir us.
Trimmed away old-fashioned Christian beliefs,
scraped off the dead bark of "meaning"

or answers located "out there."
Yet insisted both heartwood and sapwood
thrive most on intimate local community.
Tapped the rich syrup of ritual,
symbol, and myth.
Created a blend of science and spirit
uniquely suited
to Fountain Street Church.

## A Change of Perspective

the actor pivots onstage
slings sweat from his brow
shatters my willing suspension of disbelief
as does the spray of saliva
that highlights his passionate speeches

the clunk of ballet shoes on boards
draws attention away
from the delicate grace of the dance
as the clack of bassoon keys
distract from their music

but my hopes remain high
for Beethoven's "Eroica"
"the greatest symphony of all time"
when I'm placed at the orchestra's rear
in overflow seating

where the first hammer-blow chords
from this vantage thrill me afresh
main motifs I predict
surrender to subtler themes
barely perceived in the past

oboes and flutes and French horns
lay bare their souls
as the allegro slowly works back
to the tonic source
a last gorgeous burst from the brass

the stately funeral march follows
(performed unprompted in Boston
when JFK's death was announced)
its somber tones in London tonight
return me to that day

a new theme enters on tiptoe
violins surge into a fugue
work themselves up to a tempest
then whisper away
with the gentle return of the oboes

the third movement a scherzo
as witty and quick as its name
pianissimo to fortissimo
piccolo here plucked strings there
and three hunting calls from the horns

the last movement's finale
a cascade of chords descending the scales
a discordant vortex
that swells to a roar
as it tumbles into the coda

a final sequence of thunderbolt chords
lift me out of my chair
leave me breathlessly riding
the crest of a musical wave
a peak experience

## Remembering Joe

*For Joe Hansen, 1964-2019*

How his vitality livened our lives,
distinguished him from Dawn's friends
ever since the two met at fourteen.

How we envied that hair of his,
its common light brown so springy
and thick it seemed almost alive.

How cruel his parents' rejection
when he came out at sixteen,
moved into the room next to Dawn's.

How they opened their mutual wounds
to each other, promise they'd marry
if ever both ended up single.

How often the mornings he woke her
with cold grapefruit juice and funny/sad tales
of the weekend's adventures.

How lovely their laughter floating downstairs—
and every so often a muffled murmur,
a soft susurration of tears.

How selfish, sarcastic, and sensitive he could be.
How endearing and maddening in equal degree.
Each end of the gamut evoking an image:

of the delight on his face when I exclaimed
(still annoyed after dressing him down)
"You know that I love you as my own daughter!"

and of my fury—affection's dark underside—
when he absconded: stiffed me for rent,
bequeathed me the outrage of his trashed room.

Yes, that memory chafes. But it's his laugh—
as infectious and hard to defy as a yawn—
that lingers as balm to bruised thoughts.

What a torrent, that laugh—what a rich spill of sound!
Its burble carried, unchanged,
though the currents of time.

## Independence Day

*"It is time to throw out our exceptionalism and learn to be humble." –Rev. Marta Valentin*

Ours is a house built on bones,
painted to a high gloss
but swarming with termites
behind its façade.
Others' houses are no less afflicted
but humble enough not to boast
of superlative structure.
Whereas we in the land of the free
and the home of the brave
celebrate blind to the piles of sawdust
and deaf to the crunching of wood.

It needs disinfecting, this house.
Disingenuous holidays stripped,
rooms re-equipped to contain
a People of the Americas Day.
With community dances
instead of explosions,
with bonfires lighting the darkness—
finally to crown the good
with neighborhood
from sea to shining sea.

## September 12, 2001

Mocked by a brilliantined
sun against blue
as TV spews its horrors

like rivers of lava that can't be outrun,
patriotic sentiments snuffed years ago,
flare anew.

They burn hottest when fueled by music:
by the first chords
of "The Star-Spangled Banner."

By the now-shattered image evoked
by "America the Beautiful,"
"Thine alabaster cities gleam."

By the hymn set to *Finlandia*:
"My country's skies are bluer than the ocean,
And sunlight streams through clover leaf and pine."

Lyrics and music trigger an upsurge of tears,
tighten my throat, flood my chest
with a welling of love for my homeland.

How little time is required
to quench this fresh fervor of mine.
How soon I am forced to confront

the bombastic preamble to bombs,
the body parts canonized by the draped flag,
a new generation of men

that shows itself deaf to those final *Finlandia* lines:
"But other lands have sunlight, too, and clover,
And other skies are just as blue as mine."

## Archaeology at St. Gabriel's Church

To picture the past is not to look back
but to delve: to view time in vertical tiers.
Take Walm Lane, NW London today,
where legions of Romans once marched
on an already-old Celtic trail:
still a main route but now graced
with a Gothic-style church
at the end of St. Gabriel's Road.

One Sunday I step
into the full-bosomed hug
of a woman of color,
an ambient warmth on a chill summer day.
A theater stage,
rows of red-cushioned chairs,
electric guitars, piano and drums,
soft-rock praise songs.

An Anglican church, nonetheless,
which suggests Holy Writ,
the Book of Common Prayer,
the English Hymnal of 1906
along with the deeper strata
of peasant tithes paid in goods
to the medieval church,
the traditional cycles of mystery and miracle plays
performed each year from wagons
that rolled town to town.

Congregational song returns me to now,
tuneful lyrics projected on screens.
Raised arms, dreamy sway,
I the one stable sailor aboard a slow-rolling ship.
Young vicar with sticking-out ears
invites testimonials—How Jesus helped me
this week, What I'm thankful for today—
until his small son toddles up,
clings to his leg.

Almost eerie, these gentle customs,
when linked to the original
with a glance down from above:
to the middens of Roman Britain,
sherds of amphorae
and sacrificed-animal bones.
To peat-preserved bodies,
ritual sacrifices by Druidic priests.

History that speaks from the deep.
Like the seed in the rubble
of King Herod's hall
that grew into a date palm.

## Cathedral on Fire

*For Roxy*

A photograph captures a scene,
but only a painting illumines:
Picasso's Guernica.
Goya's Third of May.
Calamity somehow converted to greatness
by the strokes of a brush.

Like your painting of Notre Dame as it burned:
sky ablaze in a halo of sunset and smoke,
spire lit with flame that reduced it to bones.
Horrific, heartbreaking,
yet wrapped in such beauty
it arouses, conjures emotion
beyond its own scope:
the topless towers of Ilium torched.
Chief Joseph, his heart sick and sad.
De Gaulle's cry: France is not alone!

In the out-leaning walls on both sides
of your Notre Dame
I catch hints of the jelly-like tilt
of Van Gogh's Church at Auvers:
a slight fairytale aura to both.
Your painted cathedral, on fire,
serves to quicken my fancy,
allows me to superimpose on the buttresses
an impression of water-spouts
spewing blue spray,
to imagine the gargoyles squinting at me

through the smoke.
Though I always return to the spire aflame,
in its surrender the dominant symbol
of sorrow and loss.

Long ago, in a state of fatigue
that erased inhibition,
indifferent to tourists, self-image, dirt,
I stretched out to sleep
on its black-and-white checkerboard floor.
Not near as surreal as the shock of the fire,
the memory of that occasion,
comes alive again in your painting.

Along with rekindled respect
for this virginal vessel still pregnant
with effigies, carvings, and crowns—
a grande dame in extremity
giving birth to other great art.
Your painting reminds me
that art, even in devastation
can subpoena a species of joy
that supplants the event it portrays.

*Illustration by Roxanne Hanney: "Notre Dame Burning"*

## At the Van Gogh Museum

Thick-spread paint gleams as if fresh,
brushstrokes laid lavish.
Surprising, his range:
pear trees, peasants, poplars, potatoes,
and sunflowers, sunflowers, sunflowers:
chrome-yellow.

Always painted himself as artist:
burning eyes, concave cheeks,
rough red beard, hat bravely perched
atop poor bandaged ear. "I believe
in the art of the future," he said.
More apt, my misreading: "I believe
in the art of the face."

His propped palette
poignant in Plexiglass case:
cheap paints darkened with time
(seeming to mirror his darkening spirit)
from tubes he squeezed flat.
Their toxins perhaps puppeteers
of his madness.

Window scenes speak of a spirit
locked in pain beyond physical pain.
Still, humor grins from a skull
with teeth clamped on a lit cigarette.
Not the caution to smokers
we moderns imagine; rather, a poke
at the musty traditions applauded in art.

No suicide, as we believed, was Van Gogh.
No suicide angles a shot at his belly.
No suicide lacks powder burns on his hands.
No suicide orders more paints
after shooting himself.
New science suggests
he was shot by a youth
who had mocked him for days,
disappeared that very night.

My last stop, a still life:
work boots flopped wide at the top
to expose inner darkness,
these boots warped by weather,
by time. Stand-ins for the artist, for art:
dynamic in motionlessness.

## Our Only Immortality

*For Chris Hoffman*

A student in my mythology course,
mugged and beaten in downtown Grand Rapids
by thugs who covet his leather jacket,
dies of an aneurism.
How can I walk into class
and talk about mythological deeds,
heroes' deaths and rebirths?

I cannot.
What does mythology mean to our lives?
is the question I pose.
Personal stories matter more than great battles:
after all, I did not suspend class
when the Gulf War broke out.
Personal stories of people who move us:
Achilles, "who would not live long."
Odysseus, who wept for his men and for home.
Anne Frank, mythologized now,
who held that most humans are good.

Still, we must grapple with death,
wring from it personal meaning.
Shakespeare believed we live on in our children
and in the art of a sonnet.
True for him—
yet many, like Chris, and like us,
neither reproduce nor inspire with beauty.
All we can know is that people who die are not lost
so long as they live on in memory.

I say these things to assure them
that myths tie the personal to the universal,
offer meaningful patterns
when plumbing the implications of death.
Later papers confirm I've helped them to process
what happened to Chris.
Helped everyone but myself.

## The Eye of the Beholder

Grotesque human faces
with animal features believed to reveal
moral nature and personal worth
sketched by a Renaissance artist:
as distasteful in its assumptions
as phrenology's mirthfulness-bumps,
or physiognomy's bloodshot criminal eyes.

How not to link beauty with merit?
Painted perfection to represent virtue,
foulness and horror to symbolize vice.
Diversity, touted today as a value,
more successfully voiced than achieved.
Facial features still made cartoonish.
Birth defect, mutilation, or scarring glimpsed
rouse revulsion masked quickly as pity.

"The Ugly Duchess,"
a striking study in hideousness,
mocks the vanity of an old woman
who flirts as if young.
Portraits of Charles II of Spain
reveal a deformed Habsburg jaw,
show the price of inbreeding.
Modern busts sculpted of dismembered dolls—
baby buttocks for lips,
Barbie-legs for hanks of hair,
while still-intact dolls,
dipped like candles in beeswax

unstrained of flotsam,
solidify to the likeness of smallpox survivors.

Disfigurement as a subject for art:
merely to challenge, to shock?
Perhaps to bring the unseen out of hiding,
push for a greater acceptance,
a new definition of natural.
To show that whatever exists in the natural world
cannot be unnatural—
that imperfection, despite Keats's claim,
is often more truthful than beauty.

## Pythagoras Knew

*There is geometry in the humming of the strings,*
*there is music in the spacing of the spheres.*
*-- Pythagoras*

I cannot forget those spiky-edged
Buddha-bugs of the Mandelbrot set
whose magnified prickles unfurl
into branched lightning bolts,
the spirals and swirls of DNA.
A sacred geometry found
in art, architecture, and natural forms:
Hokusai's curling wave,
Pollock's fractalized spatters,
the Vatican staircase in Rome.
In the dazzling mandalas of monks,
mental patients, and medicine men.
In the whorled grace of a shell.

From a microverse boundlessly tiny
to a macro-reality never depleted,
an infinite world symbolized
by the god Indra's Net of Jewels:
a cosmic lattice of glittering gems,
every facet reflected in all the others,
one melodious symphony.

A Bohemian mystic* imagined creation
as a collection of mirrors
designed to reflect back to Himself
God's infinite self-replications.
I'd choose the Mandelbrot Buddha

(also resembling a cactus, a cockroach,
a cat, or a hunkering human)
to image creation,
its harmonies echoing in the vibration
of "strings" of electrons and quarks
and the inaudible songs of the spheres.
I'd choose a universe
governed by Nature alone,
expressing itself like a fractal,
never exhausted,
and endlessly lovely.

**Jakob Böhme*

## Sculpting History with Words

*America est patria mea.*
That Latin sentence in high school
aroused no shudder in me,
no shadow connected to dwindling empire.
Nor grasp of the potency of what derives
from *patria mea*:
a feminine pronoun and noun for "my nation"
that leads to "paternal," "patriarch," "patriot."

My father's mandated role, like his father's,
was to pour his child's malleable wax
into polished molds of his making.
A ranked family scheme—"family"
from *famulus* (servant or slave).
A hierarchy from in medieval times
as armature for the whole of creation:
a ladder of value descending from God.
As God governs the world, so father the family.

Fashioned from the more pliable clay
of the Latin *humanitas*,
the following Age of Enlightenment
sculpted a vessel far better suited to family use.
Hierarchy replaced with respect for all people:
women and children, couples or singles—
a container for raising children
with form matching function.

In an Age of Endarkenment
dominance soothes the scared child in the psyche

who craves a strict father to keep her secure,
a ruler who offers a semblance of safety.
Just as a bas-relief carving of Atlas
sustaining the world
preserves the illusion of depth.

Thus words that seem fragile as glass
will work with a sculptural skill
on the cellular plastic of brain,
apply chisel and rasp to reshape it.
My antidote to the Endarkenment
returns me to high school Latin:
*Encompass meum ut gens orbis terrarum.*
"May my my nation encompass the globe."

## Rainbow

We glimpse it in waterfall mists,
in a pearlescent shell
or the sheen of a puddle.
Its ephemeral presence is brief
as the deity's pledge,
obscure as the courier from ocean to cloud
who brings on the rain.
As untouchable as a mirage,
as groundless as fabled gold,
it glimmers, a vision.
Soars high.
Vanishes into the place we are not.

How deceptive the promise
of MLK's line from Theodore Parker:
the moral arc of the universe bends toward justice.
Parker's own moral eye
reached "but little ways"—
but was still full of hope

for the vivid light under a rainbow,
whose colors dim, whose clarity fades
in the sinister flicker of torchlight,
the spray-painted slurs on the door,
the flash of white officers' bullets
that shatter black bodies.
We watch as the treasure under the arch
recedes and recedes
from wherever we are.

Eyes do extend “but little ways”
to a physical arc made only of raindrops
so fragile even a feather could float
through its prismatic light.
The moral arc is as fleeting,
as insubstantial if seized—
yet as real as the sunrise,
as real as the Spring.
As a rainbow, which always returns.

## Let There Be Color

> *Van Gogh resonated to the harmonic vibrations of color like the tines of a tuning fork.*
> *–Leonard Schlain,* Art and Physics

God said, "Let there be light,"
which is color.
God's children took over:
limited commoners' clothing to brown and black,
permitted red, gold, and silver to nobles
but royal purple only to kings.
Today's nod to the impact of color
are team uniforms, national flags,
wedding whites, and funeral blacks.

Words for color in disparate cultures
are born in particular order
to the family of color terms:
white and black the original pair,
red their intrepid firstborn:
the primary pigment of civilization—
the red of passion, blood, the war god Mars,
red the fire that purifies, warms, and destroys.
A family trio of primitive power,
flaunted by Shakespeare like favorite kin,
by Hitler like orphans in swastika garb.

Cultures add words for color as couples add children,
birth order tracking the spectrum of visible light.
Yellow or green follow red.
shades of blue are the late-in-life infants,
born unbreathing or carried past term.

Ancient Hebrew and Greek
never birthed these blue babies:
Homer's seas are always "wine-dark,"
no blue at all appears in the Gospels.

Ah, poor blue,
the sometime black sheep of the family:
the blue code of silence, the blue screen of death.
Tint of cyanide, obscenity, asphyxiation, deep cold.
In masculine code words, deprived of sex.
Until the blue of a flame
and the blue of a star
proved hottest of all.
Its bad reputation reversed.

## Walls

Walls announce a need of defense,
broadcast a fear of the other,
appear unaware how easy
to be spied on by drones.

Walls wear fear-faces like chimps,
flaunt their physiques like pro-wrestlers.
Point a physical finger
to signal the walls in our heads.

Walls protest too much.
They're informants who whisper of surplus
when others are desperate.
They're impotent stallions who trumpet virility.

Walls are privileged white males,
knights at the tilt in a counterfeit battle,
narcissists full of themselves,
preachers of brimstone and fire.

Walls are hoarders amassing anxieties,
jamming the doors.
Walls daily remind us
that we are afraid.

## Visionary Eruptions

*Thanks to Keith Thompson's Angels and Aliens for the insight*

Ezekiel, Nostradamus, Black Elk,
Raphael, Gabriel, Michael:
holy figures witnessed at bedsides,
a hill in Ohio, a mountain cave.
Messengers winging through dreams,
numinous visions that ready recipients
for what's to come,
bring consolation and counsel,
materialize in times of distress.

Angels manifested to Gideon,
Mary and Joseph, the shepherds,
Mohammed, and Joseph Smith,
sparked trembling and awe for thousands of years.
Until people commercialized them,
made them cheap, sentimental.

Today cylindrical airships astound:
cigar shapes that hover and vanish,
or balls of light in the dark,
or saucer-like objects that streak through the sky
at incredible speeds.
Neologisms keep pace:
alien abduction,
government cover-up, Men in Black,
UFO, contactee, debunker.

Jung had it right:

entities characterized as divine in the past
now burst forth in machine-age editions.
Angels and gods the psychic projections
of comfort and hope.
Alien strangers in spaceships
of spiritual darkness unleashed.

## Men as Gods Memo

| | |
|---|---|
| FROM: | The U.S. Department of Men-As-Gods |
| TO: | The Electorate |
| DATE: | Today |
| RE: | Announcing the Anthropocene |

As members of a crucial government office,
we are proud to announce a name
for our new epoch,
the Anthropocene—
a milestone that reminds us
how far-seeing our forebears
to name us the sapient species.

Cynics decry the term "epoch"
for our 10,000 years on geology's time scale
(compared to the dinosaurs' 36,000)
that's not even as long as the margin of error
allowed in the dating of rocks.
We cite these very statistics
to testify to our dominion.

We do deeply regret
our role in mass extinctions,
woolly mammoth to dodo,
certain mosses to maidenhair fern.
Inopportune, but collateral damage
(as in "fallen to friendly fire"):
the price we pay for prosperity.

Perhaps you've heard the fable
designed to cause fright
that warns of a new Ice Age
triggered by global warming.
Where no mark remains of our mastery
but trace isotopes in the muck
on the floor of the sea.

Let us be clear: this claim as absurd
as millennial fever, the Second Coming,
a Rapture event.
Unworthy of sober dispute,
mere global-scale versions
of old horror tales told to children
to keep them in line.

## Emergence

consider worldwide myths
of how life began as emergence
from under the ground

like the Hopi, Zuni, and Navajo tales
of promiscuous, quarrelsome pre-human beings
driven up through a series of worlds

like the Mesoamerican codices
where under-earth caverns are fetus-filled wombs
where human footprints march out and back in

like the cave with a giant stalagmite of ice
that fits into the arch of the roof
rumored to shrink or enlarge with the moon

like the new theory of life incubated
not in primordial seas but rocks underground
or in iron-rich vents far beneath the sea floor

perfect nurseries when the surface of earth
was ravaged by asteroid blitzes
volcanic outbursts and gushers of lava

recent ideas provoked by the myriad forms
of microbial life unseen until now
at the bottom of boreholes, caverns, deep mines

old intuitions no longer mere myth
that life began in the deeps
and made its way to the light

## The Illusion of Smooth

> *Every valley shall be exalted, and every mountain and hill shall be made low: and the crooked shall be made straight, and the rough places plain.*
> *–Isaiah 40:4, KJV*

Your hands are so smooth,
said my hand-calloused boyfriend—
a perfection unquestioned
until I saw my skin magnified
squiggly as the pencil-marks
found in my mother's prized books.

A velvety petal,
a bolt of silk cloth:
flat facades revealed
to be rippled as corduroy,
serrated as saws,
crumpled like foil—

like one amplified hair
from the fur of the sleekest of cats
which shows keratin plates
overlaid like the scales on a fish.
In the flames of a fire,
or tectonic plates beneath mantle and crust,

in the branching tendrils of rivers,
or rapids white-frothed,
or the swirl of an ink-drop in water:
fractal self-replication in nature
splinters to fragments

from greatest to tiniest levels.

When you soar out and away,
the illusion returns.
No more earth spiked with mountains
or potholed with canyons,
no more discolored moon
pocked with asteroid pits.

Both perfect globes seen from space.

## Acknowledgements

"The Cattle Truck," *Heirlock Magazine, Vol. 1, Issue 1,* June 2019, p. 15 (online)

"#MeToo Medusa," *Sheepshead Review,* Vol. 42, No. 1, Fall 2019.

"Rampola's Grocery," *Sheepshead Review,* Vol. 42, No. 1, Fall 2019.

"The Slipcovered Couch," *Mangrove Review,* forthcoming

# ABOUT ATMOSPHERE PRESS

Atmosphere Press is an independent, full-service publisher for excellent books in all genres and for all audiences. Learn more about what we do at atmospherepress.com.

We encourage you to check out some of Atmosphere's latest poetry releases, which are available at Amazon.com and via order from your local bookstore:

*The Stargazers*, poetry by James McKee
*The Pretend Life*, poetry by Michelle Brooks
*Minnesota and Other Poems*, poetry by Daniel N. Nelson
*Interviews from the Last Days*, sci-fi poetry by Christina Loraine
*the oneness of Reality*, poetry by Brock Mehler
*Drop Dead Red*, poetry by Elizabeth Carmer
*Aging Without Grace*, poetry by Sandra Fox Murphy
*No Home Like a Raft*, poetry by Martin Jon Porter
*Mere Being*, poetry by Barry D. Amis
*They are Almost Invisible*, poetry by Elizabeth Carmer
*Auroras over Acadia*, poetry by Paul Liebow
*Transcendence*, poetry and images by Vincent Bahar Towliat
*Adrift*, poetry by Kristy Peloquin
*Time Do Not Stop*, poetry by William Guest
*Ghost Sentence*, poetry by Mary Flanagan
*What Outlives Us*, poetry by Larry Levy
*What I Cannot Abandon*, poetry by William Guest
*All the Dead Are Holy*, poetry by Larry Levy

# ABOUT THE AUTHOR

In 2002, when Sharon Whitehill retired as an English professor at Grand Valley State University in Michigan, she escaped at last from its snowy winters and moved to Port Charlotte, Florida. At the same time, she transitioned from the academic writing that had led to the publication of two scholarly biographies, one on *My Friend Flicka's* author Mary O'Hara, the other on Aztec and Navajo folklorist Frances Gillmor. First a children's book, *The Lizard Wizard.* Next she completed two memoirs. And at last she dared a genre she'd always loved but never thought to attempt: poetry. A handful of small publications followed; later two chapbooks; and now this full-length collection, *A Dream of Wide Water.* Her life, she declares, has indeed been a wide-awake dream.

CPSIA information can be obtained
at www.ICGtesting.com
Printed in the USA
FSHW011340290320
68556FS